W9-AET-799

ROLE-PLAYING FOR FUN AND PROFIT™

RENAISSANCE FAIRS

KRISTEN RAJCZAK

rosen publishing's
rosen
central®
New York

Published in 2016 by The Rosen Publishing Group, Inc.
29 East 21st Street, New York, NY 10010

First Edition

Library of Congress Cataloging-in-Publication Data

Rajczak, Kristen.
 Renaissance fairs / Kristen Rajczak.
     pages cm. -- (Role-playing for fun and profit)
 Includes bibliographical references and index.
 ISBN 978-1-4994-3722-5 (library bound) -- ISBN 978-1-4994-3720-1 (pbk.) -- ISBN 978-1-4994-3721-8 (6-pack)
 1. Festivals--Juvenile literature. 2. Renaissance--Juvenile literature. 3. Role playing--Juvenile literature I. Title.
 GT3932.R 35 2016
 394.26--dc23
                         2015022783

Manufactured in the United States of America.

CONTENTS

Renaissance Fairs around the country draw patrons of all ages and are often good destinations for families.

On the first day of a new season at a Renaissance fair, the anticipation in the air can truly be felt by those waiting for the gates to open. Cast members busily straighten their caps.

Costumers add last-minute touches to the costumes. Musicians warm up their instruments while the stage managers make sure the lights and sound are working properly. Patrons pull into the parking areas ready to leave behind their twenty-first century lives for a few hours as a princess, a wizard, or even just a simple peasant. As the gates open, families with children of all ages, groups of teenagers, and people dressed in all manner of medieval, Renaissance, and other fantastic clothing stream in. Calls of "Good morrow!" and "God save you!" greet these patrons as they begin to take in the sprawling Renaissance village filled with musicians, kings and queens, craftspeople, and delicious food and drink.

Renaissance fairs aim to entertain thousands upon thousands of people each year. To do so, the event staff must be organized, dedicated, and passionate about their work. Every person that patrons meet is in costume portraying a Renaissance character, including those selling food and working arts-and-crafts booths. This takes a lot of work for both those putting on the event and those committing to their character for the entirety of the fair's run. From the detailed costuming to training every worker in Renaissance-era speech and behavior, the effort put into creating a world full of believable role-playing cast members is immense. Still, the unique experience of being part of such an event is incredibly fun.

Renaissance fair workers also find their experiences rewarding, both personally and professionally. Young people hoping to gain confidence or practice public speaking have an excellent opportunity to do so. Aspiring artists and performers have ample opportunity to hone their skills through working at a Renaissance fair. And those working behind the scenes find careers in technology, theater, and historical research are within even closer reach. Whether it's for fun or for job skills, Renaissance fairs are the place to be!

CHAPTER ONE

JOURNEY INTO THE PAST

On May 11, 1963, the Renaissance Pleasure Faire first welcomed a crowd into a park outside Los Angeles, California. From the start, the fair was a place for people to dress up and forget about their lives for a while.

Phyllis and Ron Patterson conceived the event after hosting an after-school theater and arts program in the backyard of their Laurel Canyon home. At the time, the Los Angeles neighborhood of Laurel Canyon was a place where many artists and musicians lived and worked. Many were unemployed because of the Hollywood "blacklist"—a list of actors, musicians, directors, writers, and other creative people who were suspected of being communists in the 1950s. The Pattersons were lucky in a way to have begun their event at such a time. Many actors, writers, and singers were looking for places to perform. Since the Renaissance Pleasure Faire featured madrigal singers, other period music, performances, and crafts, it was the perfect outlet for a creative community unable to work much. The event was held to benefit the first public radio station, Pacifica Radio

It didn't take long for Renaissance Fairs to catch on outside California. This image shows the Colorado Renaissance Festival in the mid-1970s.

L.A., and three thousand people attended. The Pattersons' son Kevin later wrote, "The English Renaissance provided focus, but the spirit of the Faire came into being through the craftspeople, actors, musicians, and 'commoners all' who 'let the world slip' and joined the dance."

WHAT'S THE TIMELINE?

The Renaissance was a time period after the Middle Ages in Europe when the values of classical Greece and Rome became highly regarded. Art, literature, invention, and exploration all saw great developments during this time as people called humanists believed it was every person's duty to be educated.

The Renaissance lasted from the fourteenth century to the seventeenth century. That's three centuries long. It also took place all across Europe. That gives Renaissance fairs a long time period to cover. The Pattersons' fair focused on the Elizabethan age, or the time when Queen Elizabeth I ruled England, from 1558 to 1603. Her reign coincided with the Renaissance reaching England. A specific style of dress and speech is associated with the Elizabethan age, and the Pattersons' Renaissance fair was very faithful to it. Every actor and worker had to attend workshops to learn how to really live like someone from the Elizabethan era while at the fair.

GET THEE TO A FAIR!

Modern Renaissance fairs have a lot in common with the first fair that the Pattersons planned. Booths showcasing a variety of Renaissance and medieval crafts have goods for sale and also highlight the artisans who make them. Metalworking, woodworking, and leather craft are just a few skills that might be on display. Concessions selling food typical of the period are a big part of the festival, too. Music and other types of performances happen at different points of the day, as do jousts and other kinds of combat. These are some of the most popular fair events.

Most Renaissance fairs today focus on the Renaissance in England, but with the growth of Renaissance fairs, the exact time period that a fair is faithful to has become less important than entertainment in many cases. It's recognized that many fairgoers don't know much about the Renaissance and just want to enjoy the ambience.

Renaissance fairs and festivals put on by members of the Society for Creative Anachronism (SCA) focus their events on the Elizabethan era in England as the first Renaissance fair did. However, the SCA's website states that the "SCA encompasses over 1,000 years of history from pre-17th century Europe and the cultures that influence Europe." SCA encourages its members to learn about all kinds of crafts and styles from

Queen Elizabeth I's reign is often referred to as England's Golden Age. This period largely serves as the inspiration for modern Renaissance fairs.

different cultures of the Middle Ages and Renaissance. This gives workers and attendees a broader historical time period to draw from for role-playing.

Some Renaissance fairs put on workshops and provide information for attendees specifically intended to teach about the Renaissance period. Other fairs are more casual about the guidelines of the world they've created. One frequent fair worker, Steven Karscig of Pittsburgh, Pennsylvania, even noted, "As far as historically accurate representations go, one would be better off visiting a museum or taking a history class or two."

WORLDWIDE RENAISSANCE

There are hundreds of Renaissance fairs in the United States each year. Millions of people attend them. The Maryland Renaissance Festival alone, which has been around since 1977, reports 280,000 guests per season with more than six hundred performers and workers. The Ohio Renaissance Festival draws 150,000 to 200,000 people. And the United States isn't the only place hooked on these festivals! Australia is home to the Abbey Medieval Festival and the Balingup Medieval Carnivale. Denmark has the European Medieval Festival, and Greece has the Medieval Rose Festival. Many more exist in France, England, Germany, and other countries.

DO YOUR RESEARCH

Even though many Renaissance fairs and festivals keep their historical era fairly broad, knowing a bit more about the time

A variety of activities captivate audiences at Renaissance fairs, including battle reenactments such as the one shown above.

period is advantageous to fairgoers and workers alike. Today, that's easier than ever!

By using the Internet, anyone can research both the European Renaissance and Renaissance fairs. Of course, information about the time period can be found in online encyclopedias, articles from reputable organizations such as PBS, and on websites hosted by colleges and universities. Many of those tools can provide detailed information about the food people ate, the clothes they wore, the political climate of Europe at the time, and more. Ask a teacher or parent to help you find well-researched sources.

MEDIEVAL TIMES

Renaissance fairs often run for a few weeks or several weekends at a time. Some travel the country, while others have a permanent home in one location and open only seasonally. But Medieval Times Dinner & Tournament operates all year long! With nine locations across North America—including in Atlanta, Chicago, and Toronto—Medieval Times caters to families, students, and all fans of historical reenactment. It first began in Majorca, Spain, in 1973 and moved to Florida ten years later.

At Medieval Times Dinner & Tournament, patrons are brought into the eleventh century for a four-course feast and a medieval tournament, complete with real horses. A royal court presides over the meal, the most impressive of which are the "knights" that ride the horses. The knights' role at the Medieval Times Dinner & Tournament is the most well known and likely most coveted. Not everyone can be a knight! Knights need to look and act the part.

Twice a year, young men who wish to be knights at Medieval Times head to Texas to train for six to eight weeks. Their course includes horsemanship, fitness, and other skills the knights need during the Medieval Times performance. In an article for the *Gwinnet Daily Post*, a knight named Clint Mally said he had to run and do push-ups and pull-ups. "You can be a great guy, but if you can't do it physically you're wasting their time," he said.

The training needs to be tough. Being a knight at Medieval Times requires a lot of stamina. There's also the possibility

MEDIEVAL TIMES (CONTINUED FROM P. 13)

of getting injured. The weapons, which are accurate replicas from the time period, weigh four to eight pounds and include swords and axes that can actually hurt someone should they trip or mess up a fight scene or joust. Falling off a horse is another possible way for knights to get injured. However, the risks are worth it to many knights.

Others less interested in the history of the Renaissance and more concerned with their fair experience can turn to the Internet, too! In fact, there are specific forums and websites dedicated to teaching those who take part in Renaissance fairs. These sites may give an overview of the time period as well as give tips for attending a fair or festival. The SCA provides a document on their website specifically for those getting ready to attend their first event.

Renaissance fair enthusiasts are connecting on social media and message boards, too. Many devoted fans create Pinterest boards of information and ideas about Renaissance fair crafts, clothing, and food. With a parent or teacher's help, you will be able to find many Twitter accounts and Facebook groups dedicated to Renaissance fair life. These often help fair attendees and workers, new and old, keep their experience fresh. They may even make connections that can help them find the perfect Renaissance-style sword or skirt, or even a new friend. Be sure to keep personal information about yourself private when talking to others on social media. Even when sharing a common interest, being safe online should always be a concern.

CHAPTER TWO

PREPARING FOR THE ROLE PLAYERS

Before the knights don their armor and musicians tune up, those who run Renaissance fairs and other similar festivals have a lot of work to do—and for some of the bigger festivals this work may be year-round.

Work for the next year's festival often begins at the present year's festival with securing artisans and vendors for the following year's fair. Entertainers like jugglers and musicians are asked whether they'll return if their work has been satisfactory. The staff will often meet and talk about what worked well at the fair and what could be changed for the better the following year. Some Renaissance fairs own the land on which they hold their event, but others rent from a city or county and must be sure the space is available for the fair to continue. And that's just the beginning!

Once the dates of the newest season are secure, public relations and advertising can be considered. Some Renaissance fairs have a designated public relations professional who speaks to the media, conceives community tie-in events, and generally

Fairgrounds are generally the site of Renaissance fairs. Some fairs stay up year-round, but most are built each season, only to be taken down after the fair ends.

promotes the fair. The head of public relations for a fair needs to have a level of passion for his or her work that matches that of the huge fan base that can be attracted by Renaissance fairs. A love for the arts and theater are helpful when speaking about Renaissance fairs, but perhaps the most important quality is an ability to communicate well across multiple platforms.

Twitter, Facebook, Instagram, and YouTube have become a prime way to reach a large, young audience quickly and easily. Online contests for fair tickets, videos of performers getting ready, and other Internet outreach can help generate interest in an upcoming fair. It also stimulates a sense of community among festivalgoers who interact with the event and each other on social media. Some fairs have begun offering tickets at a discount on sites such as Groupon to bring in new guests, too.

FUNDING THE FAIR

In early summer 2014, the Sterling Renaissance Festival in central New York was in trouble. More than $300,000 of funding fell through, leaving festival owner Doug Waterbury to look for ways to gather the money. A combination of a bank loan, donations, and a loan from a festival patron quickly replaced the lost funding. Waterbury told Rochester, New York's *Democrat and Chronicle* that the festival had been investing profits for years and is working toward being entirely self-sufficient in the near future.

The Sterling Renaissance Festival's model isn't the only way Renaissance fairs are funded, however. Some, like the Alabama Renaissance Festival, are paid for through the fees vendors pay to be part of the festival. Others are funded by county arts programs or the National Endowment for the Arts grants, such as the Village Renaissance Faire in Wright-stown, Pennsylvania.

No matter how they're funded, Renaissance fairs are expensive to put on. Depending on the size of the festival, they can cost thousands of dollars or even millions! According to the *Democrat and Chronicle*, the Sterling Renaissance Festival cost $3 million to produce in 2014. The budget of a Renaissance fair may include the cost of renting land, permits for building

BEHIND THE SCENES

Picture this: You're walking around the local Renaissance fair with your friends and you need to use the bathroom. Who takes care of that? Modern conveniences such as parking and the presence and maintenance of bathrooms are two big behind-the-scenes jobs at an event like a Renaissance fair. There are many other jobs that need to be done that patrons often don't see:

Lights and sound Performers in any planned shows, such as the joust, need to be seen and heard by the guests. Technical professionals who often have a background in theater or concert lighting or sound are hired to make sure each performer is lit and heard properly.

Stage manager This man or woman often calls the shots backstage at the major entertainment pieces of the fair. He or she communicates with the cast, lights, sound, and even ushers in the audience to coordinate the parts of a show. Stage managers often start working toward their position as early as middle or high school while working on student productions.

Costumer Big Renaissance fairs have many people working to coordinate and create costumes for the cast members, which sometimes number in the hundreds. Since everyone from concessions workers to the queen needs a costume, the costumers have a lot to do! Throughout the festival, cleaning and repair becomes a big focus for these accomplished sewers and designers.

Box office Many fairs have a whole team in charge of selling and taking tickets who make sure the money brought in is secure and handled properly. Those in charge of the box

Working at a Renaissance fair can be tiring. Workers not only have to get their specific job done, but they must also continue to act as Renaissance villagers at every moment!

office may have a background in finance or accounting.

Food From managing the kitchens where the food is prepared to selling the food to hungry patrons, being involved with food at a fair can be a tough—and hot—job. The cooks are experienced, but some of the youngest fair workers are those working in concessions.

Construction At fairs that own their own land and have permanent buildings on it, repairs must be done before each season begins. In addition, stages, booths, and other buildings and tents must be erected before guests arrive. Due to safety concerns, experience in construction or stagecraft would be extremely important for these workers.

structures such as stages and buildings, and licenses for handling food and sometimes alcohol on city or county land. Additionally, a Renaissance fair may pay for costuming and training its workers. Training for all positions is often several weekends long.

THE PLAYERS

When King Richard's Faire in Carver, Massachusetts, was holding auditions for its 2015 season, it placed an ad on http://www.backstage.com, a well-known source of audition information for actors. The ad stated that the event was looking for men and women over age eighteen to be "village cast members; musicians (trumpeters, violinists, pipers, drummers, keyboards); singers; dancers; acrobats; actors and actresses; jugglers; stilt walkers; aerialists; street performers; specialty acts; and musical comedy performers." In a Renaissance fair, those workers who entertain and interact with the event patrons in a role-playing capacity are called the cast.

The casting for a Renaissance Fair is a lot like choosing actors for a play. People come in and may dance, sing, or do improvisational comedy games to show their quick wit and thinking. The fair's entertainment director is largely in charge of choosing who will be cast. There are small roles, such as villagers who walk around the lanes. There are big roles, such as the king and queen or those cast members who perform in scripted shows during the day. Depending on the acting experience of one who auditions and how big the part is, those in a Renaissance fair may or may not be paid.

ARTISANS AND ARMOR

An artisan is someone who has a specific skill, often done by hand. Leatherworkers, metalworkers, and woodworkers are just some of those you'll find at a Renaissance fair. Many people visit the fair just for their unique, handcrafted goods. Artisans who showcase their work at Renaissance fairs often work for years to be great at their craft.

Would you like to learn a Renaissance- or Middle Ages–era skill? The SCA offers "Arts and Sciences" classes in calligraphy, cooking, needlework, and more. True experts in these areas demonstrate and teach others, so new artisans may be able to be part of the artisan community at a fair—or just in their spare time. Those working at an artisan's booth at a fair might be learning the skills showcased there.

The SCA has activities focusing on combat, too! During the year, tournaments and even large-scale battles are put on for potential knights to hone their skills with a sword and armor. Experiences like this can help someone be chosen for a fighting role at a Renaissance fair later. Combat training can begin for children as young as five or six. Then, once old enough (age depends on the fair), an aspiring knight can become a squire, helping a knight in a joust or combat in the lanes.

Many fairs offer an apprentice program for young actors to get more theater experience. Often these programs are for those eighteen and up and can be used for college credit, much like an internship.

Remember that all performers stay in character throughout the run of the fair. Asking one about something in the outside world is considered rude!

Some artisans, Renaissance fair workers, and habitual guests are part of groups called guilds. They might include all those who role-play as Irish or do a specific craft, like wood-working. Guilds aren't easy to get into and may require a lot of work preparing for and during fairs. However, having high standards for guild entry helps make the fair experience even better. All of this work is to make sure the backdrop of the Renaissance fair—a Renaissance-era village—runs seamlessly in order for the cast to do what they do best: entertain guests!

CHAPTER THREE

AT THE FAIR

Renaissance fairs strive to be immersive experiences. Everyone who works at a Renaissance fair who interacts with the public must be dedicated to playing a role consistent with that fair's historical time period. In addition, many Renaissance fair attendees completely take on a role as well. These enthusiasts are known as "playtrons," or patrons who are playing along with the Renaissance fair cast. Both groups often spend a significant amount of time developing their characters. Playtrons often spend so much time working on their characters, they are as big a part of the festival experience as the paid cast!

FINDING YOUR ROLE

First, playtrons and cast members choose names. This is often based on the culture and time period a person is most interested in. A character with a Scottish background will have a different name than one from Italy! Playtrons and cast members can choose based on their personal interests in a culture or area

Dedicated playtrons may easily be mistaken for cast members!

Next, a character's social status and profession must be established. Both of these inform what someone's dress and behavior at the fair will be. Peasants dress simply in drab colors, but a duke or baroness might wear finer fabrics and carry himself or herself with a dignified air.

The number one piece of advice for new playtrons and cast members is to get into it! One's commitment to a character helps others stay in character, too. One way to do this is to truly flesh out a character. Building a history for a character can help one stay in that character in all fair interactions. For cast members, this has to include real reasons to interact with fair attendees. Are you a cobbler looking to help people fix their shoes? Are you a pirate who needs a crew? Having a character motivation will make fair conversations easier.

The role-playing aspect of Renaissance fairs is a big draw for many people. Renaissance fair historian Rachel Rubin wrote for KCRW.com, "Many visitors and workers have told me what they relish most about the experience is being taken out of the time and space they usually occupy—which they call their 'mundane' life—in that special place called 'faire.'"

BLENDING IN

For many "rennies"—or dedicated Renaissance fair workers and playtrons—successfully executing their character's costume and speech are a big part of the fair experience. Both aid in creating a memorable experience for all who attend.

At many Renaissance fairs and festivals, period clothing—or "garb" as rennies call it—can often be rented. For playtrons, especially those experiencing a fair for the first time, garb can simply be leather shoes, neutral-colored blouses and dresses, and snug pants. But costumes can also be quite elaborate, especially if the character someone chooses to play is a noble! Fairs tend to draw fans of fantasy literature as well, so as peasants, merchants, and nobles abound, there also may be those dressed as fairies or characters from books like *The Lord of the Rings*. Since most fairs and festivals are somewhat vague in the time period they're portraying, as long as attire is roughly from the fourteenth to the seventeenth century, playtrons will be accepted as part of the world.

Preparing for roles by studying characters from the works of Shakespeare is a great idea—Shakespeare wrote during the Elizabethan era.

Depending on the festival, the cast may have a costumer who is a stickler for historical accuracy. He or she may endeavor to use fabrics, patterns, and styles from an exact time period. Playtrons, too, may take their costuming seriously. In many cases, this means making their own garb! Costuming classes and costuming or sewing guilds are very helpful—as is YouTube and other Internet sources.

Like anachronistic dress, someone speaking in twenty-first-century American English immediately takes others out of the world of the fair. Many websites, such as the SCA's, offer tips on how to speak at a Renaissance fair. Elizabethan pronunciation, vocabulary, and grammar can be found in many other places, too. Those new to Renaissance fairs are encouraged to practice as much as possible—that's how it will eventually seem natural!

Choosing your character's background wisely can make this easier, too. Steven Karscig doesn't use an accent as his character, simply because he can't keep an accent at an all-day fair. "I usually explain this by stating, 'My dear, when you have been to the Americas as many times as I, the need for propriety in speech, holds no accord.' People usually laugh at this," Karscig said.

Karscig compared playing his Renaissance fair character to "Halloween every weekend in the summer." He has been attending Renaissance fairs since 2003. In that time, he's attended numerous fairs and worked at the Pittsburgh Renaissance Festival, the Ohio Renaissance Festival, and the Great Lakes Medieval Faire. He's been a front gate attendant and worked at booths and with vendors who sell Renaissance-style

THE SOCIAL HIERARCHY

Renaissance fairs have their own internal culture, including two distinct social hierarchies. The first is obvious—in Elizabethan England and other Renaissance cultures, the government was a monarchy, so sitting at the top of the social pyramid is a king and queen. The king and queen might hold court at certain parts of the fair day and are attired in colorful, rich fabrics making their station clear. Nobles, such as dukes and duchesses, will also be dressed to fit their station. Everyone at the fair must show reverence, or bow to, such high-ranking characters. The knights and merchants are below the nobles, and, of course, the peasants are at the bottom.

However, Renaissance fairs often have another form of hierarchy among those who work there, based on experience. Many who aspire to be a featured performer or desire a certain role are

Becoming a knight at a Renaissance fair takes a lot of work, just like earning a knighthood would during the Renaissance.

expected to work their way up. From greeting people at the front gate, one might then befriend someone who runs a craft booth and work with them at the next fair. While someone moves from job to job and from fair to fair, they gain experience, strengthen their character, and likely learn some skills they can put to use in their potential position. To become a jouster or a knight, for example, someone has to be a squire first. Then, he must go to a special jousting school or class and finally apply for the position. This could take years.

Hard work toward a goal is generally admired in the fair community. "You need to earn respect there by trying to promote this type of entertainment and establishing some sort of skill set," Karscig said. This includes those who want to become king or queen at a festival. Acting experience is required, especially if some of that experience comes from prior Renaissance fairs or similar events.

goods and crafts. Karscig, like many rennies, has been playing as his character for years. As Syrac (pronounced "SEER-ihk"), Karscig is a scholar whose main desire is to help others have a good time. Karscig can describe Syrac in depth, including his relationship to playing the character: "Syrac as a character is difficult to get away from for two reasons: one, some people at faire and on the circuit know me by his name and appearance, and two, I have played him for so long, unfortunately the character and I have become very similar when interacting in the faire setting."

Beyond the Cast

Everyone who interacts with the public at a Renaissance fair will be playing a role, complete with a costume. Young people who work at concessions or taking tickets at the gate get to be part of the fun, too! Positions like these are where a lot of teenagers begin their work at a Renaissance fair. These may be volunteer positions or paid, depending on the fair. Either way, they're great opportunities to decide if the rennie life is for you.

For young people just starting out, Renaissance fair life can be a big shock. The fair must go on, rain or shine, and in very hot and very cold weather. The hours are often long, and interacting with playtrons can be exhausting—even for parking attendants! It can also be very rewarding, especially for the young workers who find a home within the family of Renaissance fair workers. Often, older artisans, actors, and behind-the-scenes workers will act as guides for the new, younger workers, helping them navigate the tough days and find ways to have fun in their character. It's these relationships that keep many Renaissance fair cast members and workers coming back each year.

AFTER THE FAIR

The possibility of a career working at a Renaissance fair depends greatly on what kind of job you'd like to have. Many people who work behind the scenes at Renaissance fairs—including business managers, entertainment directors, producers, and the communications staff—have a position working on the fair year-round. When the fair isn't in it's active season, they perform a regular job with regular hours, just like a teacher or nurse would have. But, for most people, working at Renaissance fairs isn't a lucrative career path. That doesn't stop dedicated rennies from making a serious hobby of traveling the circuit of fairs, especially during the summer, though!

USING YOUR SKILLS

Renaissance fair work, whether paid or not, can provide excellent experience for other careers. Even as a hobby, working at a Renaissance fair helps establish many good skills, especially for young people.

RENAISSANCE FAIRS

Those looking for acting and performing experience find intense training working at a Renaissance fair. Not only do cast members have to stay in character for many hours at a time, they're not often bound by specific lines of dialogue or a certain scene. Instead, they greet playtrons and patrons in character and see where a conversation takes them. Improvisation in character helps future actors learn how to commit to a character truly and also how to think and respond quickly. With such long days at the fair, problems are sure to arise, and cast members are often on the frontlines, finding ways to handle any situation in character—just as they would if something went

Experience in stage acting or drama club can be particularly helpful for somebody hoping to work at a Renaissance fair.

wrong on a stage in a play or on live camera!

Costumers and make-up artists who help ready the cast for the public receive excellent training for jobs in theater and television, too. Set builders and sound technicians also have clear paths into theater work. Cast members who take a great interest in the dialects used when portraying a fair character might use those skills to coach or teach other performers, or even groups of second-language learners.

Renaissance fair work often requires a bit of research and understanding of the Renaissance as a time period. History

If you have a passion for history and researching day-to-day life in the past, a career as a history teacher or professor is a great option for you.

teachers and historians put research skills to good use. Someone with a great interest in the Renaissance might look for a career that allows him or her to use historical information actively, such as a professor of Renaissance literature interpreting writing from that time. Someone who wants to pursue work as an archivist or museum curator would find the study of Renaissance clothing, food, and entertainment excellent preparation. It's often very detail-oriented work to

VIRTUAL ROLE-PLAYING

Going to or working at a Renaissance fair is just one way to role-play as a medieval knight or a king from the Renaissance. Many RPGs (role-playing games) allow players to be transported back in time to close to the same time portrayed by many Renaissance fairs. Many even strive to be historically accurate! *Kingdom Come: Deliverance* and many games like it take players to medieval Europe, fleshing out the world of the game with clothing from the actual time period, true-to-life armor, and combat techniques of the time. Some of these games include fantasy aspects, such as magic, while others don't. Since fans of the fantasy genre and rennies are often one and the same, characters from popular games are common costumes at Renaissance fairs.

Do you enjoy RPGs *and* Renaissance fairs? As technology continues to advance, new games are always in development. You could use the research you've done to develop your Renaissance fair character to create a whole new RPG, perhaps starring your character! Renaissance fair experiences would truly aid an RPG developer, as playtrons and workers already have the enthusiasm for disappearing into a role. Applying that passion to the story of a game would show through. It would be likely to attract other Renaissance fair lovers, too!

Those who aspire to a career in video game development often need more than passion and a good idea, however. Consider adding to your Renaissance fair skills by learning about computer coding, digital artwork, and even writing

Video game development is another great career for somebody with a passion for role-playing. You can build your own fictional world for yourself and others to live and act in.

dialogue. Doing even more research about the Renaissance through history classes helps, too. Just like at the Renaissance fair, a video game needs to be set in a whole world for players to discover!

make the Renaissance village as historically accurate as possible. This work would easily translate to the close study of documents and artifacts in libraries and museums.

Even as a young person, you can start finding ways to incorporate skills learned working at a Renaissance fair into your career path. Becoming an apprentice with a Renaissance-focused artisan can lead to exploring other kinds of art, such as jewelry making or pottery. Helping the costumer create the cast's garb aids in organization, sewing, and an understanding of fabric and fit. Aspiring fashion designers could learn a lot! Experiences as a cast member could of course give a young actor or actress plenty of practice. But the constant public speaking and quick thinking develops skills useful for lawyers, teachers, and even politicians, too! Being part of the social media team or other managerial support positions gives great experience to those wishing for a career in communications, public relations, or any position that requires coordinating people. Much of the behind-the-scenes work of Renaissance fairs is great for a future event planner to observe as well!

PEOPLE SKILLS

When sitting for a job interview, you may be asked a lot about yourself and your experiences. Even if you've never had a paid job before, activities, volunteer work, and even time spent working at a Renaissance fair can help you answer! Renaissance fair workers have to spend a lot of time interacting with the public. This gives you a specific set of skills valuable to every employer you'll meet—people skills.

As a Renaissance fair worker, you'll learn to communicate well with just about anyone! This is because, first of all, so many people are involved in putting on a Renaissance fair. You'll likely work with managers, long-time employees, and support staff. You'll learn to take direction from your superiors and communicate any difficulties you may find while at work. Without good communication between people running a Renaissance fair, the event will fall apart. This knowledge and practice will be helpful in any workplace.

Renaissance fair workers interact with patrons of all walks of life and all interest levels. You'll be an adaptable communicator from your experiences at a fair. From greeting dedicated play-trons willing to role-play with you to trying to explain where the bathroom is to a family with young children while in character, you'll be able to confidently tell a future employer that you can successfully navigate all kinds of social situations. Additionally,

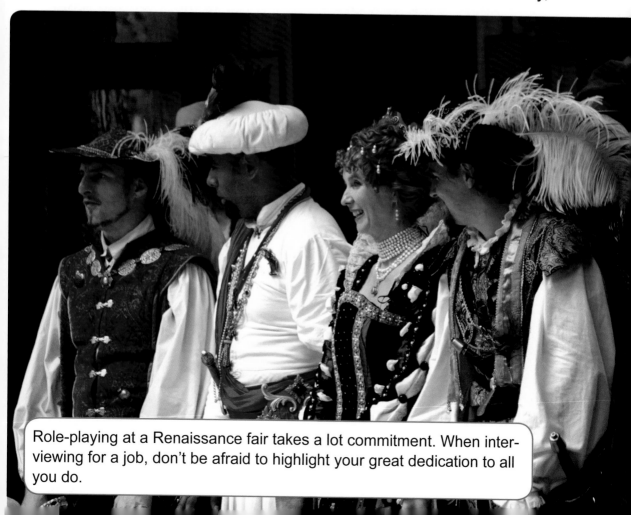

Role-playing at a Renaissance fair takes a lot commitment. When inter-viewing for a job, don't be afraid to highlight your great dedication to all you do.

employers will be impressed with the conflict and resolution skills you'll have from these many interactions in the lanes. Among all the patrons you meet, not all of them are going to be happy!

Finally, Renaissance fair workers must be tireless and willing to give their all. As a young person, this can be easy because you already have lots of energy! But, as you enter your career, having enthusiasm for every task you need to do can be hard. Practicing keeping your energy and positivity high at a Renaissance fair can be really helpful when your job gets stressful.

Getting a job at a Renaissance fair is just like any other place of employment. You have to apply! Begin by looking on the fair's website to see when they are taking applicants. Consider getting in touch with someone you know has worked there before, too. Most young people begin work as parking attendants, concession sellers, kitchen workers, and greeters. However, with enthusiasm and motivation, you can move up to larger cast or behind-the-scenes positions within a few seasons! Is working at a Renaissance fair for you? Don your feathered cap or your peasant's dress and find out!

ambience The mood or feeling of a place.

anachronistic Having to do with anachronism, or something from one time period placed incorrectly in another.

apprentice Someone who learns a skill by working with an expert.

audition A try-out for a performer.

calligraphy The art of making beautiful handwriting.

circuit A series of events held in different places over the course of a time period.

communist A person who supports communism, or a society structure in which the government owns what is used to make and transport products and citizens don't own anything privately.

hierarchy The series of levels a group of people is organized into based on importance.

immersive Fully involving or surrounding.

improvisational Having to do with improvising, or making something up as one goes along.

internship A position in which someone, usually a student, works at a job to get experience.

joust An event at which knights fight on horseback with lances.

lanes The streets between Renaissance fair stages.

madrigal A type of song for several singers and no instruments popular in the sixteenth and seventeenth centuries.

replica An exact copy.

stamina The strength that allows one to do something for a long time.

Barrie Swordplay Association
Classic Martial Arts
43 Morrow Road, Unit #1
Barrie, Ontario
Canada
(416) 822-7725
Website: http://www.barrieswordplay.com/default.html
Those who truly want to train in the combat arts for
    Renaissance or medieval festival training can do so
    here. Classes include long sword, spear, and grappling.

Belegrath Medieval Combat Society
The locations and contact information for local realms can
    be found here: http://belegarth.com/begin.php?link=map
Website: http://belegarth.com
The Belegrath Medieval Combat Society takes part in
    live-action battles in which their members can use
    real—but safe—weapons they've made and role-
    play in various ways. Belegrath chapters can be
    found all over the United States, in Canada, and in
    many other countries.

Costumer's Guild West, Inc.
1917 Crestshire Drive
Glendale, CA 91208
Website: http://www.cgwcostumers.org
Both amateur and professional costumers interested in role-
    playing costuming, including Renaissance fairs, can get
    involved with the Costumer's Guild West, Inc.

Council for the Medieval and Renaissance Faire
1739 N. High Street
Columbus, OH 43210
(614) 688-4636
Website: http://cmrf.org.ohio-state.edu
This student-run organization at Ohio State University runs
the school's annual Medieval and Renaissance Faire. For
young people interested in Renaissance fair event planning
or performance, it provides an unparalleled opportunity
for involvement.

Renaissance Society of America (RSA)
The Graduate Center, CUNY
365 Fifth Avenue, Room 5400
New York, NY 10016
(212) 817-2130
Website: http://http://www.rsa.org
The RSA is the largest international society dedicated to
the study of the Renaissance. Its over six thousand members dedicate their time to the academic study of the Re-
naissaince, publishing the *Renaissance Quarterly* jour-
nal and granting scholarships and awards annually to
dedicated researchers.

Shakespeare in Action
570 Shaw Street, Room 14a
Toronto, ON M6G 3L6
Canada
(416) 703-4881

Website: http://www.shakespeareinaction.org
Education is paramount for this organization, which hosts events, camps, and presentations for young people to learn more about the Elizabethan great, Shakespeare.

Society for Creative Anachronism
PO Box 360789
Milpitas, CA 95036-0789
(800) 789-7486
Website: http://www.sca.org
This international organization has over thirty thousand members around the world dedicated to the reenactment of pre-seventeeth century Europe. It puts on events, classes, and feasts at which skills and dress from this time period can be showcased.

WEBSITES

Because of the changing nature of Internet links, Rosen Publishing has developed an online list of websites related to the subject of this book. This site is updated regularly. Please use this link to access this list:

http://www.rosenlinks.com/RPFP/Fairs

Elgin, Kathy. *Elizabethan England*. New York, NY: Chelsea House, 2009.

Gibson, Douglas. *Tales of a Fifth-Grade Knight*. North Mankato, MN: Stone Arch Books, 2015.

Hinds, Kathryn. *Elizabeth and Her Court*. New York, NY: Marshall Cavendish Benchmark, 2008.

Kuiper, Kathleen, ed. *Musicians of the Renaissance*. New York, NY: Britannica Educational Publishing, 2013.

Lamedman, Debbie. *A Teen Drama Student's Guide: Laying the Foundation for a Successful Action Career*. Hanover, NH: Smith and Kraus, 2007.

Langley, Andrew. *Medieval Life*. New York, NY: DK Publishing, 2011.

Lawler, Mike. *Careers in Technical Theater*. New York, NY: Allworth Press, 2007.

Leventon, Melissa. *What People Wore When: A Complete Illustrated History of Costume from Ancient Times to the Nineteenth Century for Every Level of Society*. New York, NY: St. Martin's Griffin, 2008.

Murphy, Lauren. *Art and Culture of the Renaissance World*. New York, NY: Rosen Central, 2010.

Roberts, Russell. *How'd They Do That in Elizabethan England?* Hockessin, DE: Mitchell Lane Publishers, 2010.

Shone, Rob. *Elizabeth I*. New York, NY: Rosen Central, 2005.

Summers, Gillian. *The Tree Shepherd's Daughter*. Woodbury, MN: Flux, 2008.

West, David. *Richard the Lionheart*. New York, NY: Rosen Publishing Group, 2005.

Wettersten, Laura. *My Faire Lady*. New York, NY: Simon & Shuster Books for Young Readers, 2014.

Carcig, Steven. Personal interview by the author. April 8, 2015.

Cattanach, Joanna. "Hopefuls Train to Be Medieval Times Knights at Texas Ranch." Dallas Morning News. Retrieved April 4, 2015 (www.medievaltimes.com/dallas/newspress /hopefuls-train-to-be-medieval-times-knights-at-texas -ranch.aspx).

Conti, Katheleen. "From Pilgrims to Wizards, a Hub for Unique Performers." *Boston Globe*, May 29, 2014. Retrieved April 15, 2015 (www.bostonglobe.com/metro/regionals /south/2014/05/28/from-pilgrims-wizards-plymouth -carver-area-hub-for-unconventional-performers /ui4WkYQ7s9hEYx9nGCRHyM/story.html#).

Fairehistory.org. "Faire Founders," "50th Jubilee Forward." Retrieved March 10, 2015 (www.fairehistory.org).

Medieval Times Dinner & Tournament. "About Us." Retrieved April 4, 2015 (medievaltimes.com/corporate/about-us .aspx).

Plotz, John. "Zounds, Milady!" *Slate Book Review*, February 2013. Retrieved March 30, 2015 (www.slate.com/articles /arts/books/2013/02/renaissance_faires_rachel_lee _rubin_s_well_met_reviewed.html).

Renfaire.com. "An Introduction to Renaissance Faires," "Cos-tuming & Costume Accessories," "Acting & Working with the Public." Retrieved March 10, 2015 (www.renfaire.com).

Rubin, Rachel. "Leftists, Weirdies, and the Political Roots of the Renaissance Faire." Kcrw.com Zocalo Public Square blog. April 5, 2013. Retrieved March 30, 2015 (blogs.kcrw .com/whichwayla/2013/04/leftists-weirdies-and-the-political -roots-of-the-renaissance-faire).

Society for Creative Anachronism Newcomer's Portal. "History and Culture." Retrieved March 10, 2015 (welcome.sca.org /history-and-culture).

Upadhye, Neeti. "Renaissance Festival to Go On as Planned." *Democrat and Chronicle*, July 1, 2014. Retrieved April 4, 2015 (www.democratandchronicle.com/story/news/2014 /07/01/renaissance-festival-go-planned/11929627/).

Vitti, John. "Behind the Scenes at the Royal Joust." *Boston Globe*, August 29, 2014. Retrieved April 15, 2015 (http:// www.bostonglobe.com/lifestyle/2014/08/29/behind-scenes -royal-joust/sV7S6GiuBJOfg6M5VEAbUN/story.html).

INDEX

ABOUT THE AUTHOR

Kristen Rajczak is a children's book writer and editor from Buffalo, New York. No stranger to theatrical role-playing, Kristen performed in many productions as an undergraduate at Gannon University and was a member of the national theater fraternity, Alpha Psi Omega. She also received her master's degree in arts journalism from the S.I. Newhouse School of Public Communications at Syracuse University with an emphasis in theater and literature criticism.

PHOTO CREDITS